WEIRD
MAZES

William Potter
Leo Trinidad

WINDMILL
BOOKS

Published in 2019 by Windmill Books,
an Imprint of Rosen Publishing
29 East 21st Street, New York, NY 10010

Copyright © Arcturus Holdings Ltd, 2019

Written by: William Potter
Illustrated by: Leo Trinidad
Designed by: Stefan Holliland with Emma Randall
Edited by: Joe Harris with Julia Adams

Cataloging-in-Publication Data

Names: Potter, William. | Trinidad, Leo, illustrator.
Title: Weird mazes / William Potter; illustrated by Leo Trinidad.
Description: New York : Windmill Books, 2019. | Series: Ultimate finger trace mazes | Includes glossary and index.
Identifiers: ISBN 9781538390092 (pbk.) | ISBN 9781508197270 (library bound) | ISBN 9781538390108 (6 pack)
Subjects: LCSH: Maze puzzles--Juvenile literature.
Classification: LCC GV1507.M3 T756 2019 | DDC 793.73'8--dc23

Manufactured in the United States of America

CPSIA Compliance Information: Batch BW19WM: For Further Information contact Rosen Publishing, New York, New York at 1-800-237-9932

CONTENTS

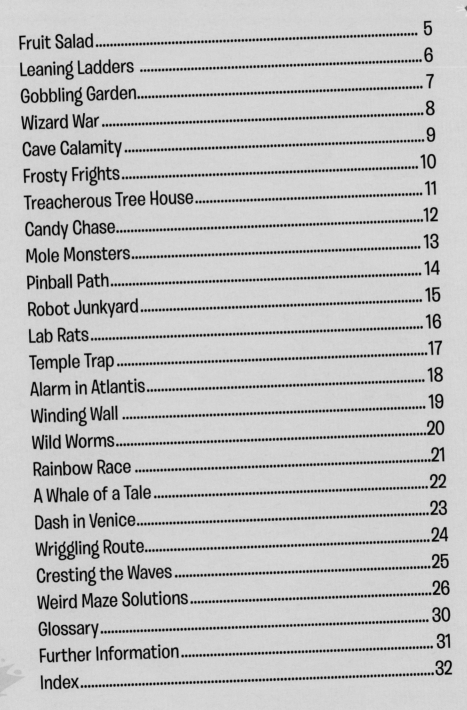

HOW TO USE THIS BOOK

This book is full of high-risk mazes, where you have to help the heroes find a safe path to complete their daring missions. Look out! Every page is packed with perils.

1. READ THE INSTRUCTIONS CAREFULLY BEFORE USING YOUR FINGER TO GUIDE THE HEROES FROM THE START TO THE FINISH.

2. AVOID ALL THE DANGERS. MAKE SURE THE HEROES AREN'T TRAPPED, ZAPPED, OR SNAPPED UP FOR LUNCH!

EXIT

SAVE HIM!

START HERE!

3. OFTEN, SOMEONE NEEDS RESCUING. LEAD THE HEROES THERE FIRST, BEFORE HELPING THEM TO ESCAPE!

4. YOU CAN FIND THE SOLUTIONS TO ALL THE MAZES FROM PAGES 26 TO 29.

FRUIT SALAD

Climb over banana bridges and the spoon to reach your stuck friend, then escape past the beastly berries.

GOBBLING GARDEN

These plants have a taste for humans. Brave your way through the maze to stop them from gulping down your friend, then get out again.

7

WIZARD WAR

Our heroes must escape a wacky wizard world without being zapped or caught by magic monsters.

CAVE CALAMITY

Look out! The cave is flooding. Help the heroes climb down to rescue their friend and bring him to the surface, avoiding creepy cave creatures.

START AND FINISH

HELP!

TREACHEROUS TREE HOUSE

Use the ropes and ladders to climb up to the jungle tree house. Be careful not to get mauled by a monkey or jaguar on the way!

CANDY CHASE

Cross the candy fantasy land past the sweet treats, but watch out for the chocolate chompers!

START

ESCAPE

MOLE MONSTERS

Can you make your way out of the terrible tunnels without meeting the monstrous moles and slimy worms?

PINBALL PATH

This kid is imprisoned in a giant pinball machine. Steer him through the game to escape without striking any bells or flickers.

START HERE!

WAY OUT

ROBOT JUNKYARD

Can you find a safe route through this junkyard, without getting grabbed by android arms? Don't reactivate the robots!

START HERE!

ESCAPE

TEMPLE TRAP

To escape the temple maze, the adventurer will have to climb up the rope. Guide the way, watching out for bad-tempered birds and tumbling rocks.

ESCAPE

START HERE!

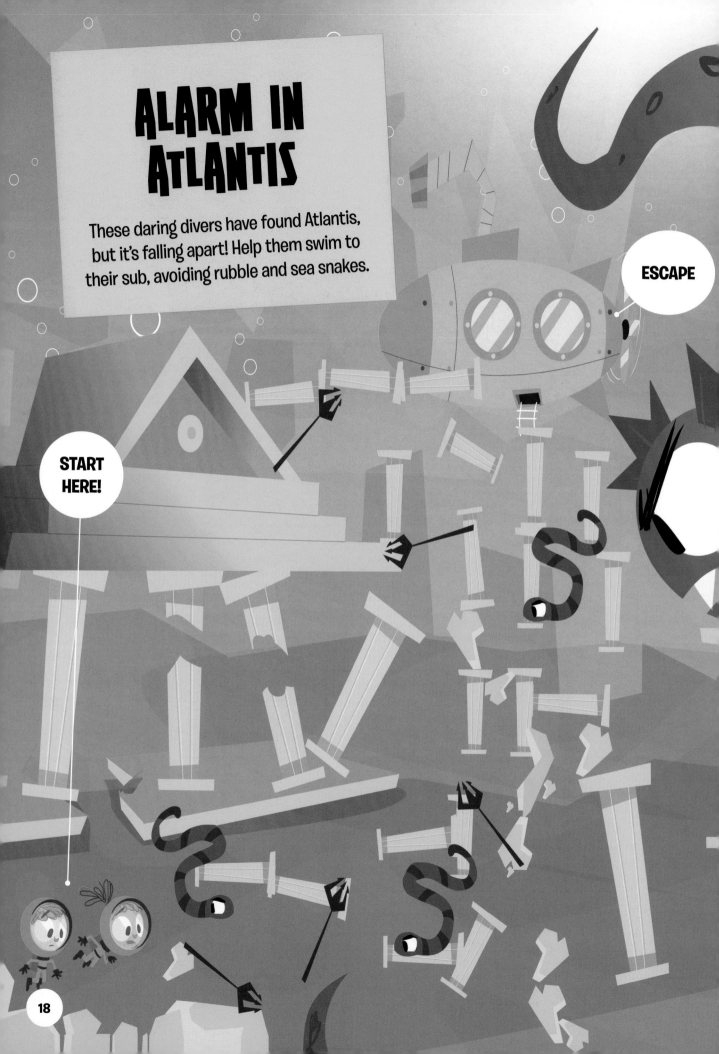

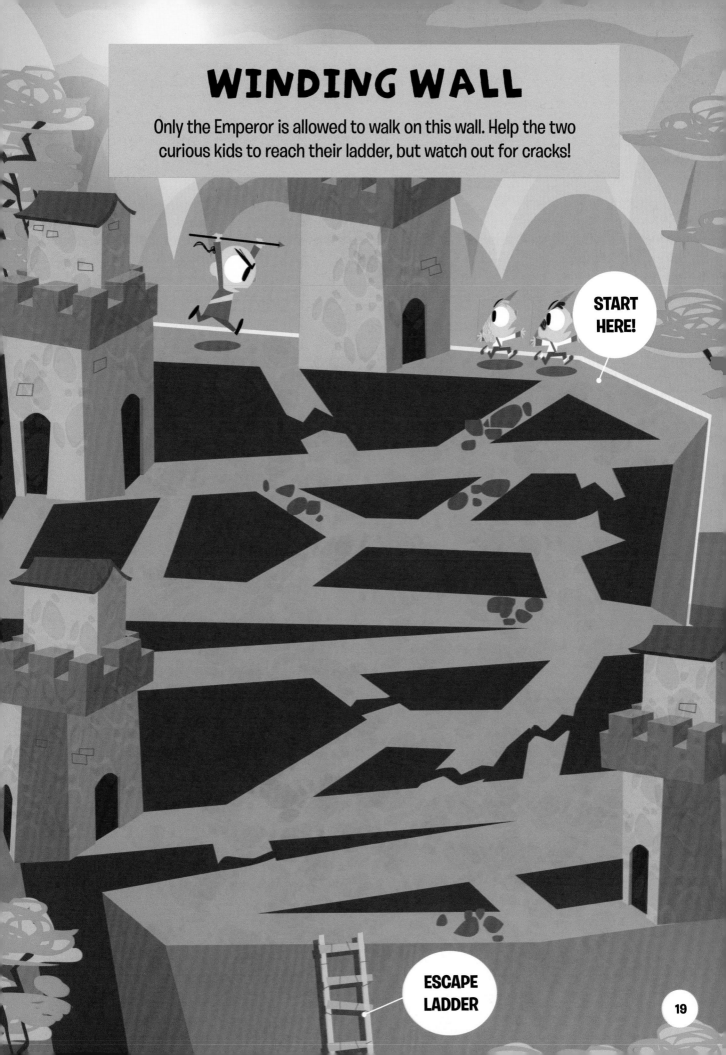

19

RAINBOW RACE

Help the cloud princess over the rainbow bridges to Earth, avoiding the lightning-throwing imps.

START HERE!

BACK TO EARTH

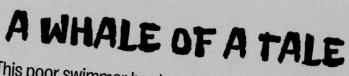

A WHALE OF A TALE

This poor swimmer has been swallowed by a whale! Help her get out of its gut, avoiding the rest of its meal.

ESCAPE

START HERE!

WRIGGLING ROUTE

These fairy folk need to catch the next butterfly flight.
Help them find a way through the munching millipedes.

FAIRY FLIGHT

START

24

CRESTING THE WAVES

This surfer is riding a huge wave. Help him reach the shore in one piece by following the path and avoiding surfing turtles.

START HERE!

THE SHORE

WEIRD MAZES
SOLUTIONS

PAGE 5

PAGE 6

PAGE 7

PAGE 8

PAGE 9

PAGE 10

PAGE 11

PAGE 12

PAGE 13

PAGE 14

PAGE 15

PAGE 16

PAGE 17

PAGE 18

PAGE 19

GLOSSARY

Atlantis A legendary island that thrived until it was submerged beneath the sea.

android A robot that looks human.

calamity An event that causes sudden and significant damage.

carnival A yearly festival that takes place in the streets of cities around the world. It usually involves parades, music, masks, and dancing.

emperor The ruler of an empire.

gelato Italian ice cream.

imp A small, mischievous fairy-tale creature.

imprisoned Locked up or trapped.

maul To wound by biting or scratching.

millipede A long insect with up to 750 legs.

reactivate To bring something back into action.

research station A settlement where scientists live while they carry out research.

restore To bring something back to the way it was.

rubble Chunks of stone, concrete, and brick.

treacherous When something holds possible dangers.

FURTHER INFORMATION

Books:

Artymowska, Aleksandra. *Amazed*. London, UK: Laurence King Publishing, 2017.

Blundell, Kim and Jenny Tyler. *Big Book of Mazes*. London, UK: Usborne Publishing, 2004.

Flintham, Thomas. *Thomas Flintham's Marvellous Mazes*. London, UK: Scholastic, 2011.

Robson, Kirsteen. *Third Big Maze Book*. London, UK: Usborne Publishing, 2015.

Websites:

For web resources related to
the subject of this book, go to:
www.windmillbooks.com/weblinks
and select this book's title.

INDEX